# Goodnight Dallas

Written by
**Jennifer Drez**

Illustrated by
**Lisa Voight**

Goodnight Dallas - walkSTEM Edition
ISBN-13: 978-0-9886023-3-5
Illustrations by Lisa Carrington Voight using acrylic on canvas.
Graphic Design by Cynthia Wahl
Printed in Canada

To order additional copies of this book, please visit www.goodnightdallas.com or www.talkstem.org

# Exploring with walkSTEM tools

*We have included some easy to use tools that will help your child be a STEM explorer. Use our Shape Finder, Angle-a-tron (a beginner's protractor) and map while reading this book or in your backpack as you travel around your neighborhood and beyond.*

Children are natural explorers, fascinated by the world around them. Have you ever noticed your child more interested in objects around the house such as pots and pans, a picture on the wall or even a speck of dust on the floor rather than in their toys? Play should be open-ended, imaginative, and fun to support children as they build their capacity to connect the abstract with the real world. At the same time, helping children become familiar with useful measurement tools is both fun and builds confidence.

Our Shapefinder and Angle-a-tron (on the two plastic inserts in this book) make learning about real-world geometry through play exciting and relevant. Your children can go on shape-finding adventures in the book, around your home, and beyond! At the end of this book you will also find a customized map and legend showing the locations of the Dallas sites you and your child will visit through this book.

**Visit talkSTEM.org and click on walkSTEM® Academy to watch our short videos to see the Angle-a-tron and Shape Finder tools at work as well as a short video on using and making maps!**

**Dear Parents and other Educators,**

We are thrilled to partner with the author and illustrator of Goodnight Dallas to bring you this walkSTEM® edition. walkSTEM® is an initiative created by the talkSTEM nonprofit organization. It is not built on a foundation of textbooks and math problems, but on real world experiences. We celebrate the meaningful connections between Science, Technology, Engineering, the Arts, and Math in the everyday world.

walkSTEM® was developed collaboratively by talkSTEM founder, Dr. Koshi Dhingra, who holds a doctorate in science education from Teachers College, Columbia University, and Dr. Glen Whitney, walkSTEM adviser and founder of the National Museum of Mathematics - the only math museum in North America.

Our vision is a world where every place is a STEM place and every child is a STEM child - excited to explore, ask questions, and problem solve everywhere they go.

We design walkSTEM® stops all across Dallas, many of which are represented in this book. At each stop, STEM explorers of all ages can ask and answer questions based upon what they notice. What can you learn about symmetry from observing turtles in a pond? How fast are you traveling when riding a ferris wheel?

Many of the jobs our children will hold do not exist today. It is critical we support their natural curiosity as they acquire the mindset primed to innovate, make connections, and inquire, all while having fun. This engaging book is a great place to start.

Thank you for reading!

Koshi Dhingra, Ed.D
Founder and Director
talkSTEM
Share. Engage. Inspire. ™

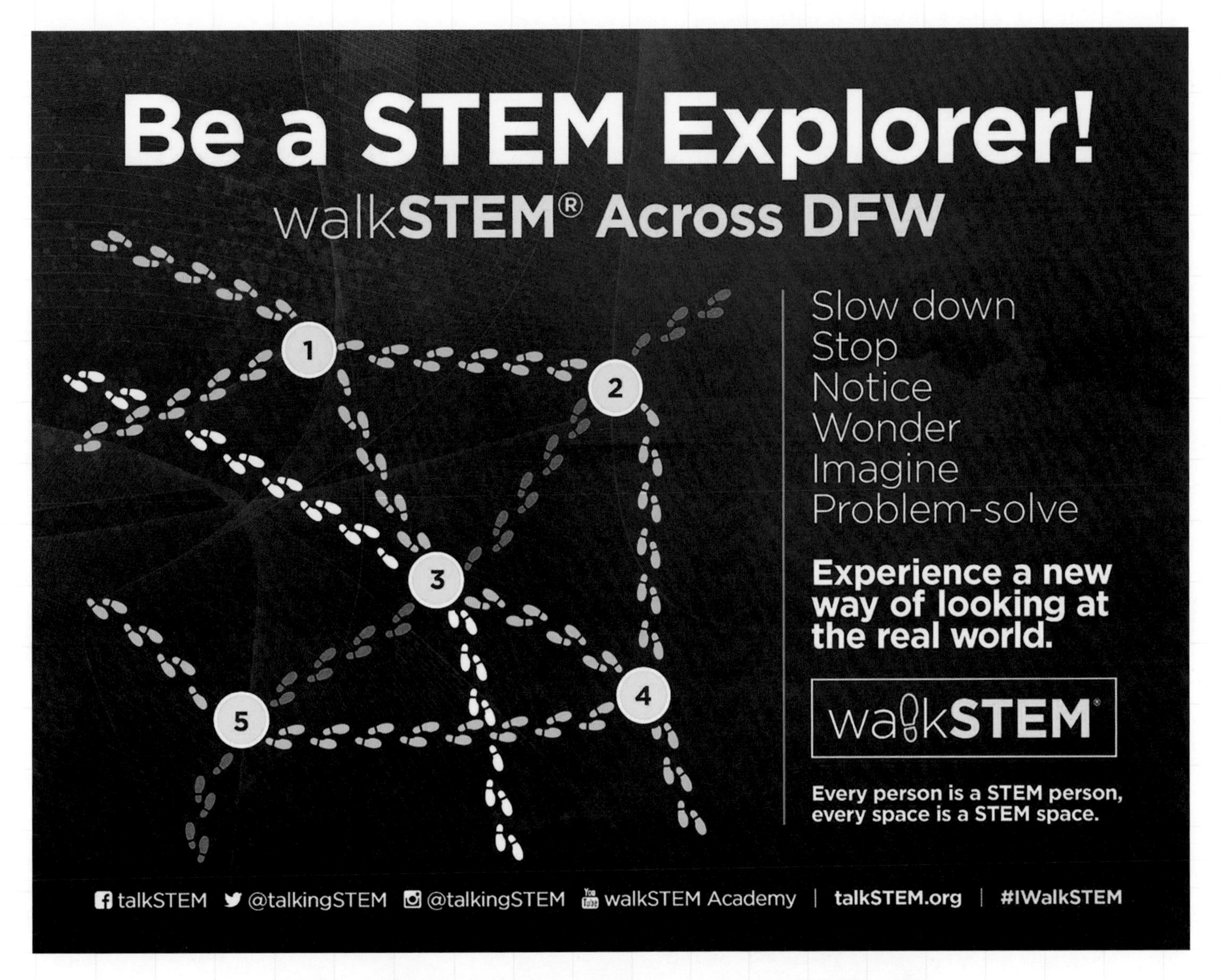


**Each yellow circle represents a walkSTEM® stop.**

**A walkSTEM® stop could be anything from a place in your home, a building, playground equipment, or a popular neighborhood site.**

**Visit walkSTEM Academy online to view our instructional videos.**

The sun is setting on the Dallas skyline.

Let’s say goodnight as the stars begin to shine.

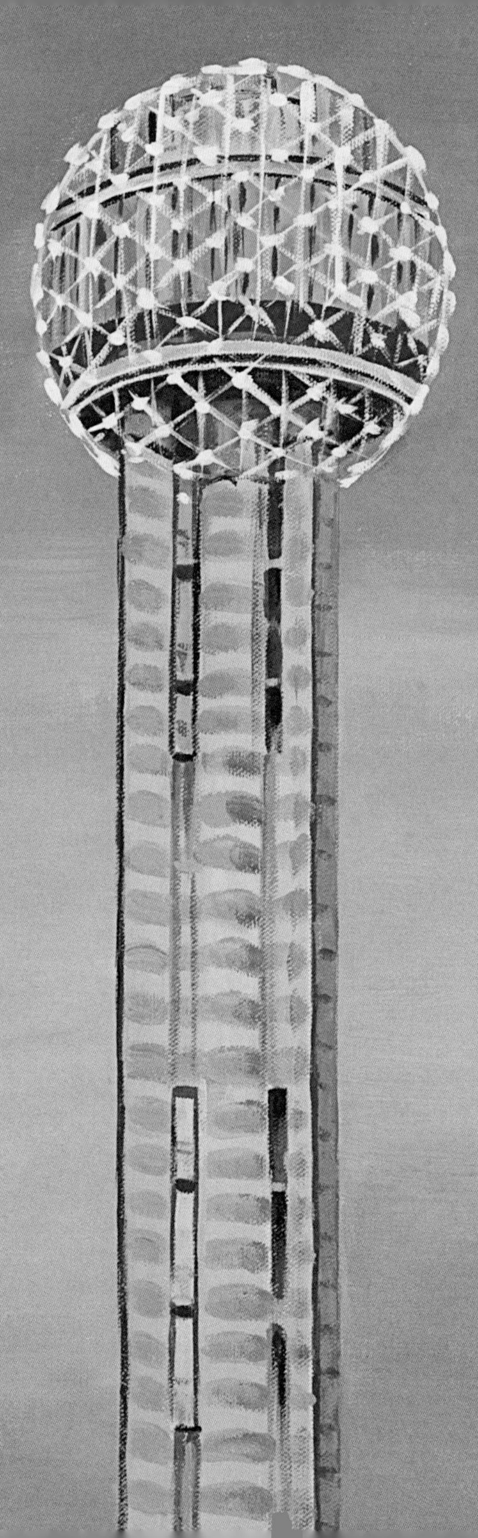

**Goodnight Reunion Tower**
**and to the Adolphus.**

Goodnight to the
Magnolia Hotel with its
flying red Pegasus.

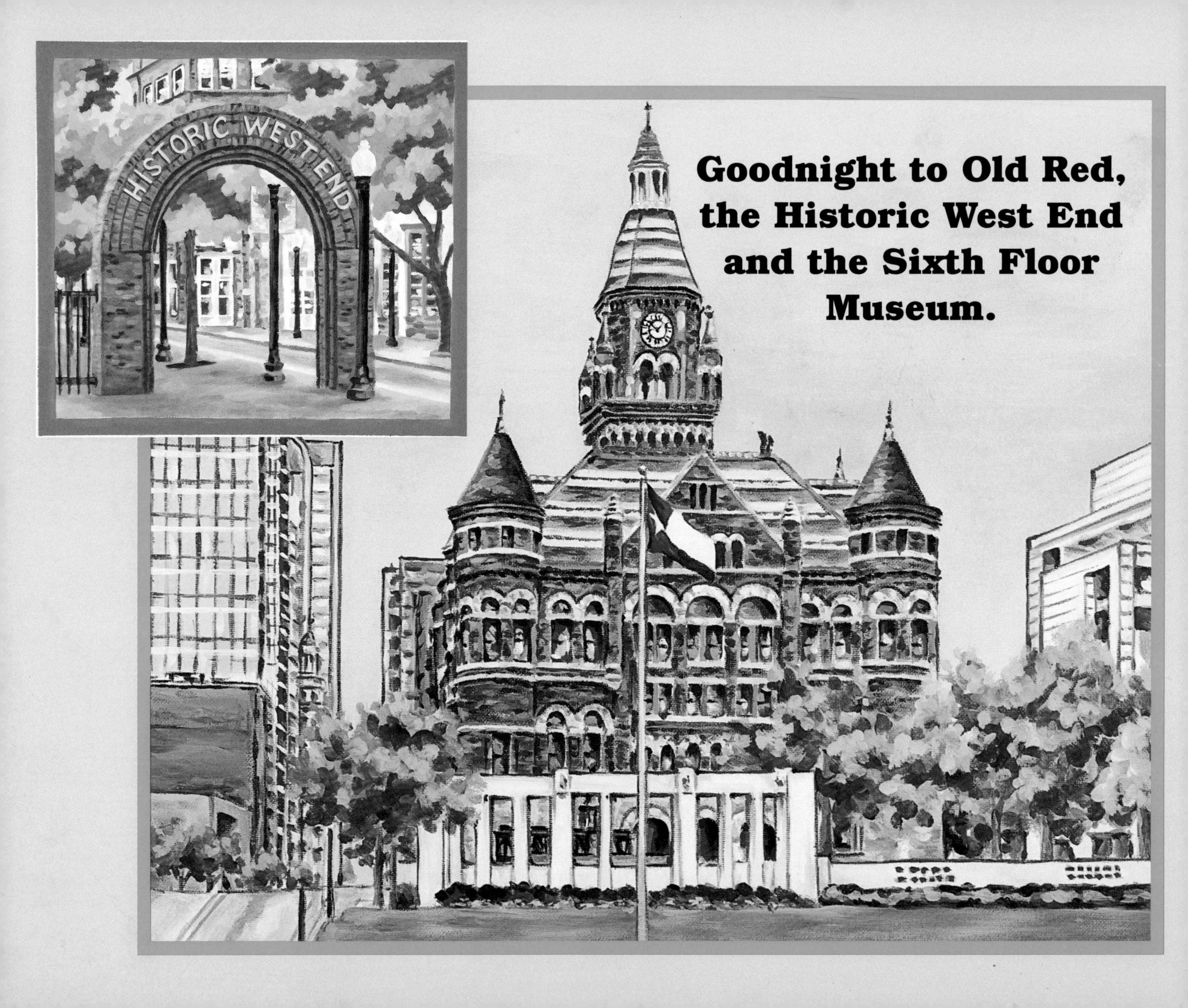
HISTORIC WEST END
Goodnight to Old Red,
the Historic West End
and the Sixth Floor
Museum.

**Goodnight to the Winspear, the Wyly and the Meyerson.**

Goodnight to the DMA, the Crow Collection
and the Nasher's amazing sculpture.

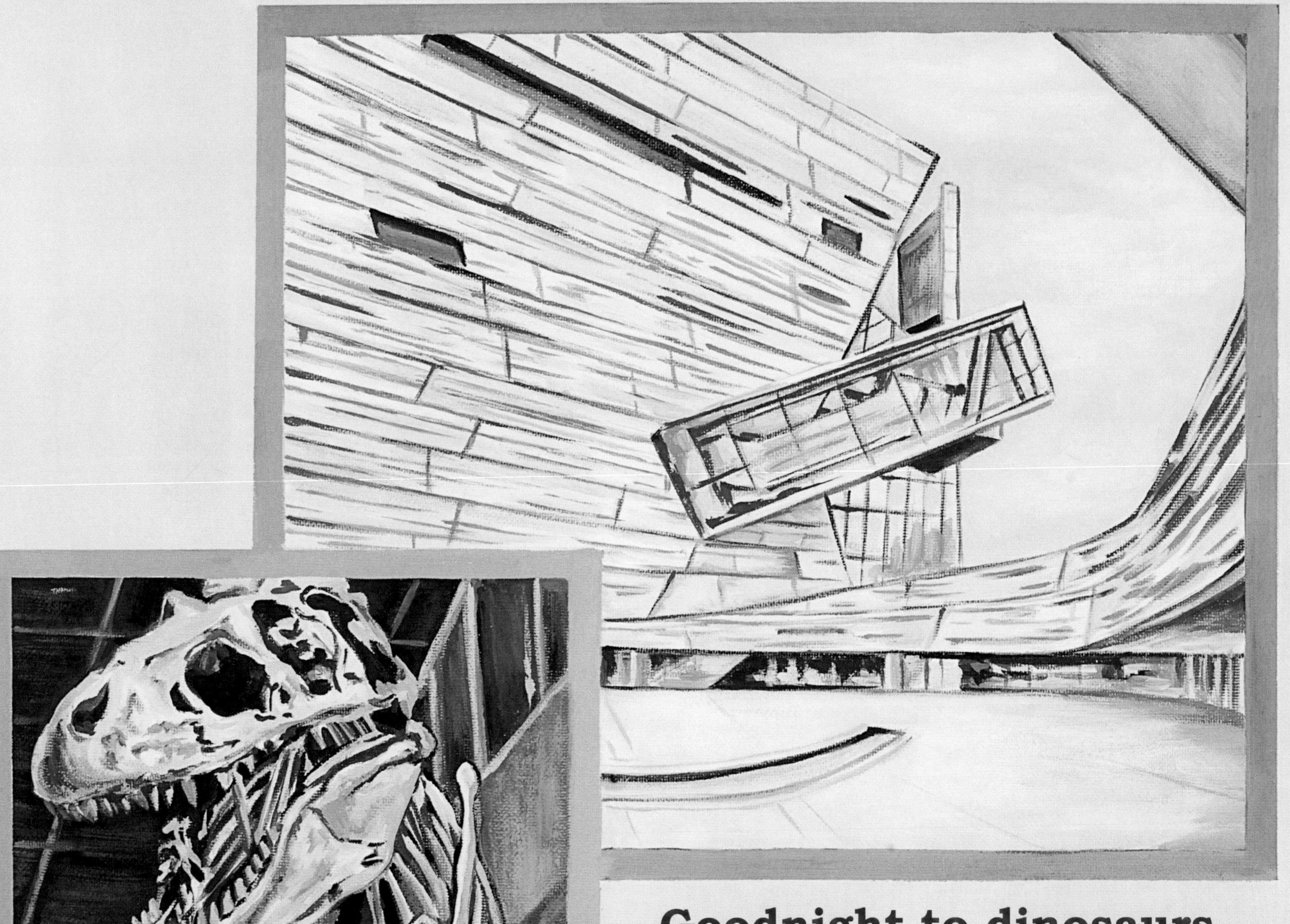

**Goodnight to dinosaurs,
musical stairs and
inspiring architecture.**

Goodnight to Klyde Warren Park where we exercise, eat and play.

Goodnight to the
Aquarium,
a great sloth,
sea creatures
and stingrays.

**Goodnight to fun times at the Majestic Theatre and the Latino Cultural Center.**

Goodnight to the
Farmer's Market,
fruits, veggies and
flowering planters.

**Goodnight to the Bishop Arts District,**

**the Trinity River and the Margaret Hunt Hill Bridge that stands so tall.**

Goodnight to
the mayor,
City Hall, police
and firefighters.

Thank you for
leading and
protecting us all.

**Goodnight to the McKinney Avenue Trolley and to Katy Trail where we walk, skip and run.**

**Goodnight to ducks swimming in Turtle Creek, beautiful azaleas and a splashing fountain.**

**Goodnight SMU, The Meadows Museum and the Bush Library.**

**Goodnight to Kuby's, Highland Park Village and coke floats at the Pharmacy.**

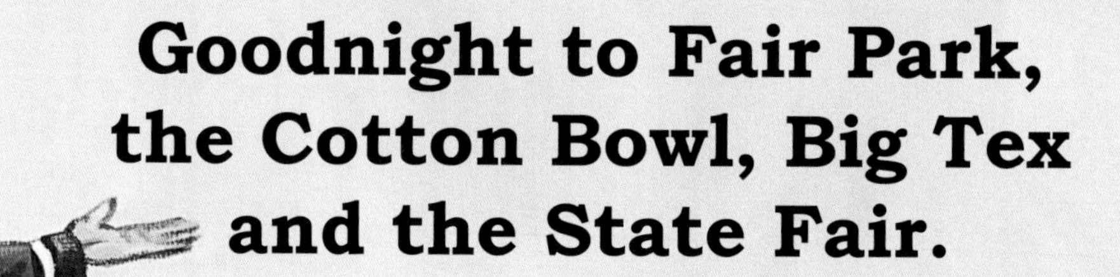

**Goodnight to Fair Park, the Cotton Bowl, Big Tex and the State Fair.**

Goodnight Pioneer Plaza,
the cowboys and
cattle we see there.

**Goodnight to old favorites: Sonny Bryan's, El Fenix, Campisi's and La Calle Doce.**

**Goodnight Love Field**
**with planes taking off to fly far away.**

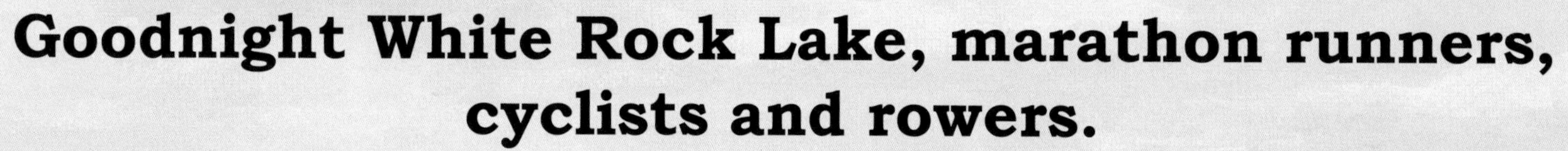

**Goodnight White Rock Lake, marathon runners, cyclists and rowers.**

Goodnight to the Arboretum,
the Children's Adventure Garden
and colorful flowers.

Goodnight
to tigers,
penguins and
giraffes at the
Dallas Zoo.

Goodnight to golfers at the Byron Nelson Championship, too.

**Goodnight to Neiman Marcus,
the NorthPark slides and
shops selling everything
from cupcakes to toys.**

Goodnight to victory celebrations for the Mavericks,
FC Dallas, Stars, Rangers and Cowboys!

The sun has set, the stars shine bright.

Sweet dreams, Dallas. Goodnight!

## A Note about walkSTEM® Academy

walkSTEM® Academy is talkSTEM's free video library where you can find short videos highlighting the STEM involved in many of the places you see in this book. You can use the QR code provided to access these videos. These videos are meant to be used as a portal to transform the conversation to one that directly involves observation and inquiry. As an additional resource, most videos have corresponding Educator/Parent Guides with suggested activities and guiding questions, available as free downloads on our website, talkstem.org, under the Educator Resources Tab.

Select the questions and talking points that you feel will best engage your child. The goal is to support them with new ways of looking at the world around them and to encourage them to come up with their own questions.

We also urge you to check out our digital forum on talkstem.org to learn more about STEM-related news and learning opportunities. We'd love to hear from you. Make sure to share your experiences on social media using #iwalkstem!

# A guide to walkSTEM® Academy

## Videos for Parents and Educators of Young Children

We recommend watching the videos separately from your children and then discussing the questions with them as you read the book or while visiting the sites in person.

**Scan me to visit walkSTEM Academy.**

*(QR Code created with QRstuff.com)*

See if you can find the page with the matching location for each of the videos listed below!

**Click on Dallas Arts District Playlist**

*Stops Highlighted in Goodnight Dallas:*

Why is there a gap in the building's facade (Wyly Theater)?
How do you measure Pitch and how is it helpful (Wyly Theater)?
How can shapes create feelings (Meyerson Opera House)?
How do artists use math to mix colors (Dallas Museum of Art)?
What's the architect's favorite ratio (Nasher Sculpture Center)
What can you measure in bamboo plants (Nasher Sculpture Center)?
What's the most symmetrical solid (Klyde Warren Park)?

**Click on NorthPark Center Playlist**

*Stops Highlighted in Goodnight Dallas:*

What types of symmetry do we see (Turtle Pond)?

**Click on Fair Park Playlist**

*Stop Highlighted in Goodnight Dallas:*

How Fast Can you Go (Texas Star)?

**Click on West End Historic District Playlist**

*Stops Highlighted in Goodnight Dallas:*

How Tall is the Arch? (Gateway Arch)
How Much Water is in the Pool? (Dealey Plaza)
How will the Roof Change? (Dallas Holocaust Museum)

If you like these videos, please click the subscribe button on walkSTEM Academy to stay in the loop about new videos!

**“Math** is one of the world's most powerful systems of problem solving. Now that computers do our calculations for us, it is applicable in almost every walk of life - to STEM and beyond. The sooner children can integrate quantitative or computational thinking into every activity as they explore the world, the sooner it becomes a natural approach for them and one that will empower them throughout their lives.”

— Conrad Wolfram
Strategic Director and Co-founder/CEO
of Wolfram Research Europe

## ACKNOWLEDGEMENTS

Dallas is a diverse, culturally rich city with a dynamic history. My goal is that this book will help visitors and residents celebrate everything that Dallas has to offer. I am grateful to the many people that helped bring this book to life. Everyone involved, including people in local government, non-profit leadership and local residents, have a great love for Dallas and pride in its history. Dallas is an amazing city to raise a family, live, visit, play and work. I hope the people of Dallas are proud of *Goodnight Dallas* and share it with others.

# DALLAS

Dallas was founded in 1841 when John Neely Bryan laid claim to 640 acres and sketched out a town plan. In 1846, Dallas County was formed and the city of Dallas was incorporated on February 2, 1856. Located on the Trinity River, Dallas quickly became the center of trade in cotton, grain and buffalo. At one point, Dallas was the world's leading inland cotton market.

The area continued to grow and attract more attention over the years. Railroads arrived in the 1870s, Neiman Marcus in 1907, the Federal Reserve Bank in 1914, SMU in 1915, Dallas Love Field Airport in 1917 and the Texas Centennial Exposition in 1936.

Over the years, Dallas became a financial center for the oil industry and is also well-known for its role in banking, transportation and computer technology. Today, Dallas is a leading corporate destination embraced for its entrepreneurial spirit, style, innovation and opportunity. Its sport teams, cultural institutions, parks and great shopping all make Dallas a favorite tourist destination.

**Reunion Tower**
This 50-story observation tower in downtown Dallas was designed by Welton Becker & Associates and was completed in 1978. It is adjacent to the Hyatt Regency Hotel and is one of the most recognizable landmarks in Dallas. Reunion Tower is known for its 360 degree observation deck with interactive activities and a revolving restaurant and bar.

**Adolphus Hotel**
Located in downtown Dallas, the Adolphus Hotel is an upscale hotel and Dallas landmark. It opened in October 1912 and is the oldest hotel in Dallas. It was built by Adolphus Busch, founder of the Anheuser–Busch Company. Designed by Thomas Barnett in a Beaux Arts style, the Adolphus has a long list of famous and notable hotel guests that includes musicians, business leaders, presidents and world leaders.

**Magnolia Hotel and the Pegasus**
This building originally was headquarters to the Magnolia Petroleum Company. It is best known for its trademark Pegasus that was erected on the roof in 1934 in celebration of the American Petroleum Institute's annual meeting. The Pegasus remains a well-known landmark and endearing Dallas icon.

**Old Red Museum of Dallas County History & Culture**
The building that houses the Old Red Museum was built in 1892 as the Dallas County Courthouse. Designed by Max Orlapp, Jr. in the Richardson Romanesque style of architecture, it was built with red sandstone with marble accents. In 1966, a newer courthouse replaced Old Red and the building now serves as a local history museum.

**Dealey Plaza**
Dealey Plaza, completed in 1940 as a WPA project, is located on land donated to the City of Dallas by Sarah Horton Cockrell. It is named for George Dealey, a civic leader and early publisher of the Dallas Morning News. Dealey Plaza is best known as the location of the assassination of John F. Kennedy on November 22, 1963.

**The Sixth Floor Museum at Dealey Plaza**
The Sixth Floor Museum is located on the sixth and seventh floors of the former Texas School Book Depository. The Museum chronicles the life, death and legacy of President John F. Kennedy. It aims to be an impartial, multi-generational forum for exploring the events surrounding the assassination of President Kennedy.

**Margot and Bill Winspear Opera House**
The Winspear Opera House, home to the Dallas Opera and the Texas Ballet Theater, is located in the Arts District. The Winspear also partners with local and national organizations to present a variety of cultural programming. The building was designed by Foster and Partners as a 21st century interpretation of a traditional opera house.

**Dee and Charles Wyly Theatre**
The Wyly Theatre and its impressive architecture was designed by Joshua Prince-Ramos and Rem Koolhaas. The theatre can seat up to 600 people and can transform into many different configurations, allowing for incredible performance flexibility. The Wyly serves as the venue for the Dallas Theater Center, Dallas Black Dance Theatre and the Anita Martinez Ballet Folklorico.

**Morton H. Meyerson Symphony Center**
The Meyerson, which was designed by distinguished architect I.M. Pei, opened in 1989. It is home to the Dallas Symphony Orchestra, the Turtle Creek Chorale, the Dallas Wind Symphony and the Greater Dallas Youth Orchestra. The Meyerson is well-known for its impressive design and unsurpassed acoustics.

**Dallas Museum of Art**
The Dallas Museum of Art (DMA) is located in a building designed by Edward Larrabee Barnes in the Dallas Arts District. The DMA's collection began in 1903 as the Dallas Art Association and now consists of more than 24,000 important objects, dating from the third millennium B.C. to the present. The Museum is well-known for its role in the community, free admission and its Center for Creative Connections.

**Crow Collection of Asian Art**
Trammell and Margaret Crow opened the Crow Collection of Asian Art in 1998 as a permanent museum. The Museum showcases the art and cultures of China, Japan, India and Southeast Asia. It is considered one of the finest museums in the United States focused on Asian Art.

**Nasher Sculpture Center**
The Nasher Sculpture Center opened in 2003 and is home to one of the finest collections of modern and contemporary sculptures in the world. Designed by architect Renzo Piano in collaboration with landscape architect Peter Walker, the museum aims to be a focal point and catalyst for the study, installation, conservation and appreciation of sculpture. The collection consists of more than 300 sculptures dating from the late 19th century to the present.

**Perot Museum of Nature and Science**
The Perot Museum of Nature and Science offers dynamic experiences to stimulate curiosity in visitors of all ages. The extraordinary building, exhibit halls and outdoor spaces all serve as living science lessons through hands-on discovery. The building and landscape design demonstrate scientific principles and serve as examples of sustainability and conservation.

**Klyde Warren Park**
Klyde Warren Park serves as a central gathering space for Dallas and its visitors. It is a five-acre urban deck park built over Woodall Rogers Freeway. The park includes a performance pavilion, walking trails, food trucks, children's park, dog park and a games area.

**The Dallas World Aquarium**
Located near the Historic West End, the Dallas World Aquarium, opened in 1992. The upper level is a reproduction of the Orinoco Rainforest, which has one of the only public displays of three-toed sloths. The lower level features aquariums with fish and sea animals from around the world and includes the Mundo Maya exhibit filled with plants and animals important to the ancient Mayan culture.

**Majestic Theatre**
The Majestic Theatre opened in 1921 and is one of the most elegant and historic performing arts spaces in the Southwestern United States. The Majestic hosts shows ranging from nationally touring concerts and comedy acts to locally-produced cultural events and fundraisers.

**Latin Cultural Center**
The Latin Cultural Center is a multidisciplinary arts center designed by architect Ricardo Legorreta. It serves as a regional catalyst for the preservation, development and promotion of Latino and Hispanic arts and culture.

**Dallas Farmer's Market**
The Dallas Farmer's Market opened in the late 1800s and continues to be a large public market in the center of the city. The market offers a wide variety of fruits and vegetables from local farmers, wholesale dealers and produce dealers. There are seasonal festivals, cooking classes, yard sales and an adjacent floral and garden market.

**Bishop Arts District**
The Bishop Arts District is a small shopping and entertainment district located in North Oak Cliff. The area is known for street festivals and a large selection of restaurants, independent boutique shops and galleries.

**Margaret Hunt Hill Bridge**
The Margaret Hunt Hill Bridge is a defining landmark of the Trinity River Corridor designed by renowned architect and engineer Santiago Calatrava. The bridge connects Woodall Rogers Freeway to Singleton Boulevard in West Dallas. It was built to spur economic development and foster unity within Dallas by connecting the North and South Oak Cliff neighborhoods.

**Dallas City Hall and Park Plaza**
Dallas City Hall and Park Plaza were designed by world-renowned architect I.M. Pei. The building is an inverted pyramid design with a reflecting pool and notable sculptures adorning the area. It serves as the seat of the city's municipal government.

**La Calle Doce**
In September 1981, Oscar and Laura Sanchez welcomed the first customers into La Calle Doce in Oak Cliff. As a twenty-year veteran of numerous restaurant kitchens, Oscar had developed a vision for a restaurant of his own featuring seafood and Tex-Mex made with the freshest ingredients. Since then, La Calle Doce has been serving visitors from Dallas and beyond.

**McKinney Avenue Trolley**
The McKinney trolley is run by the McKinney Avenue Transit Authority. It recreates the trolley system that served Dallas from the early to mid-20th century. Restored vintage trolleys provide a great way to see and explore Uptown Dallas. The car in the illustration is Car 122, Crescent Rose or "Rosie," which was built in 1909 and is the oldest streetcar in daily service in the United States.

**Katy Trail**
Katy Trail is a jogging, walking and cycling path that follows the path of the old Missouri-Kansas-Texas Railroad, known as the MKT or the Katy. The trail runs through the Uptown and Oaklawn areas and provides a way of connecting various city parks. It is funded by the Friends of Katy Trail, a non-profit organization founded in 1997.

**Turtle Creek**
Turtle Creek is a scenic tributary of the Trinity River starting in Reverchon Park and winding through Oak Lawn and into Highland Park. The creek is surrounded by beautiful neighborhoods, fountains and landscaped areas perfect for a stroll or picnic. The area is maintained by the Turtle Creek Association.

**Southern Methodist University**
Founded in 1911 by the Methodist Church, Southern Methodist University (SMU) is a highly-regarded private academic institution. The campus is home to the George W. Bush Presidential Library and Museum and the Meadows Museum. SMU's sports teams play in the Division 1 American Athletic Conference. The team mascot is a Mustang pony, named Peruna.

**Meadows Museum**
The Meadows Museum is located on the SMU campus and has one of the largest and most comprehensive collections of Spanish Art outside of Spain. The collection was amassed by Algur H.Meadows, who gave the funds to SMU to construct and endow a museum to house his vast collection as a unique resource for local schools, colleges and the community.

**George W. Bush Presidential Library and Museum**
The Bush Presidential Library and Museum on the SMU campus houses the records of the life and career of George W. Bush, the 43rd President of the United States. The collection encourages a better understanding of the Presidency and American history and provides a multi-generational, interactive and educational experience for the entire family.

**Kuby's Sausage House**
In 1961, Karl Kuby immigrated to Dallas from Germany and opened Kuby's Sausage House, Inc. in Snider Plaza near SMU. His goal was to introduce Texas to the tradition and the taste of fine specialty sausages and foods of his childhood. Kuby's recipes use only the finest ingredients and have been handed down from father to son for more than 14 generations.

**Highland Park Village**
This upscale shopping center is a National Historical Landmark. It opened in 1931 as the first self-contained shopping center in America. Its classic architecture, fine shopping and restaurants make it a great destination for residents and tourists alike.

**Highland Park Soda Fountain**
Highland Park Soda Fountain, originally Highland Park Pharmacy, opened in 1912. Locals still refer to the establishment as the Pharmacy and the best place to go for a great grilled cheese or an old-fashioned milkshake. Historical newspaper clippings dating back to its opening adorn the walls, providing informative and entertaining reading material.

**Fair Park**
Fair Park is a National Historic Landmark located on 277 acres and is the largest collection of Art Deco exposition style architecture in the United States. It is home to seven museums and six performing arts facilities, including Music Hall, Texas Discovery Gardens, Gexa Energy Pavilion, the African-American Museum and the Cotton Bowl Stadium. Fair Park has been home to the Texas State Fair since 1886.

**State Fair of Texas**
The State Fair, which started in 1886, is held in Fair Park and lasts for 24 days every year. It boasts a car show, carnival rides, football games at the Cotton Bowl, corny dogs, fried goodies and much more. The iconic Big Tex, a 55-foot tall cowboy, towers over the State Fair to greet and entertain visitors. The Fair also features the Texas Star, a 212-foot-tall ferris wheel.

**Pioneer Plaza**
Pioneer Plaza is a public park located in downtown Dallas featuring native plants and trees along with a large bronze longhorn cattle drive sculpture by Robert Summers. The sculpture commemorates the trails that brought early settlers to Dallas and cattle to the market place.

**Sonny Bryan's**
In 1910, Elias Bryan opened Bryan's Barbeque. The family tradition continued in 1958 when his grandson opened Sonny Bryan's, which is well-known for its mouthwatering barbeque. Locals and tourists alike remember the school desks that are used as dining tables in some of their seven locations.

**El Fenix**
In 1918, Mexican immigrant Michael Martinez and his wife Faustina decided to turn their modest café in Dallas into El Fenix. The restaurant is renowned as the originator of "Tex-Mex Cuisine." Generations of families have grown up dining at the historic Dallas restaurant and continue to do so today.

**Campisi's**
Originally founded as Campisi's Egyptian Lounge by Joseph Campisi in 1946, the Campisi family continues to own and operate Campisi's more than six locations in Dallas and beyond. It is said that Campisi's is where Texas' first pizza was made and served.

**Dallas Love Field**
Love Field is a city-owned public airport. It was named by the United States Army in honor of Lt. Moss L. Love. The airport officially opened in 1917 as a flight training base for the U.S. Army Corps. Today, Love Field is a thriving airport that is also corporate headquarters to Southwest Airlines.

**White Rock Lake**
Built in response to a water shortage in Dallas in 1910, White Rock Lake now serves as a recreational lake for the city. It is surrounded by trails for hiking, running and bicycling as well as the Bath House Cultural Center and the Dallas Arboretum and Botanical Garden. The lake is a popular destination for rowing, sailing and fishing.

**Dallas Arboretum and Botanical Garden**
The Dallas Arboretum and Botanical Garden is one of the top ten display gardens in North America. With 66 acres on the shores of White Rock Lake, this nationally recognized garden has changeable displays four times a year, providing breathtaking color for visitors from March through November. The Rory Meyers Children's Adventure Garden, an eight-acre interactive garden, is the only children's educational garden of its scope in the world.

**Dallas Zoo**

Offering 106 acres of wildlife adventure, the Dallas Zoo is the largest zoological experience in Texas. Home to more than 2,000 animals representing over 400 species, the Zoo provides unique interactive activities such as giraffe and bird feedings, a mini Safari Express train, and a Monorail Safari tour. The zoo also features an eleven-acre Giants of the Savanna exhibit, the only place in North America where elephants share their habitat with giraffes, zebras and other African species.

**Byron Nelson Championship**

The Byron Nelson Championship is a PGA Tour golf tournament held each spring. Named after Byron Nelson, the tournament's first winner in 1944, it is organized and run by the Salesmanship Club of Dallas.

**Neiman Marcus**

The Neiman Marcus Company was established in 1907 in Dallas as a local specialty store. The company was founded by Herbert Marcus along with his sister Carrie M. Neiman and her husband Al Neiman. Neiman Marcus Group LTD LLC operations include the Specialty Retail Stores segment and the Online segment. The Specialty Retail Stores segment consists primarily of Neiman Marcus, Bergdorf Goodman and Last Call stores. The Online segment conducts direct to consumer operations under the Neiman Marcus, Horchow, CUSP, Last Call and Bergdorf Goodman brand names.

**NorthPark Center**

NorthPark Center was opened in 1965 and continues to be one of the premier shopping centers in America. The Center is a top tourist and shopping destination and features unique art as well as fun family activities such as the NorthPark slides, large sloped planters that children love to play on. Generations of children in Dallas have memories of running up the planters and sliding down while taking a break from shopping.

**Dallas Mavericks**

The Dallas Mavericks are members of the Southwest Division of the National Basketball Association (NBA). Since their inaugural season in 1980-81, the Mavericks have won three division titles, two conference championships and the NBA championship in 2011.

**Dallas Stars**

The Dallas Stars are a professional hockey team in the Central Division of the Western Conference of the National Hockey League (NHL). The Stars have won seven division titles, two President's trophies, two Western Conference Championships and a Stanley Cup Trophy in 1999.

**FC Dallas**

A member of Major League Soccer since its inception in 1996, FC Dallas is owned and operated by Hunt Sports Group. FC Dallas formerly known as the Dallas Burn soccer club, claimed the U.S. Open Cup in 1997 and earned its first Western Conference Championship in 2010. Renowned for its youth development system, FC Dallas is known for the "home grown" Dallas talent on its professional roster.

**Texas Rangers**

Originally franchised in 1961, the Arlington-based Texas Rangers are members of Major League Baseball's American League. Fans have enjoyed cheering them on to five AL West division titles and two AL championships.

**Dallas Cowboys**

The Dallas Cowboys are a professional football franchise playing in the East Division of the National Football Conference (NFC) of the National Football League (NFL). The Cowboys joined the NFL in 1960 as an expansion team. Five-time NFL champions, the Cowboys have had eight Super Bowl appearances and are the most valuable team in the NFL. They are the only team to record 20 straight winning seasons (1966-84).

**“Fostering** the creative spirt in our children is essential to enhancing their daily lives. Children who develop their powers of observation enrich both a deeper understanding of the world around them and the artist within them. Learning to observe deeply requires new techniques for visual learning as they identify details, connect new ideas, and transform this information into creative responses connecting the arts and sciences.”

**— Bonnie Pitman**

**Distinguished Scholar at the University of Texas at Dallas and the former Eugene McDermott Directorof the Dallas Museum of Art**

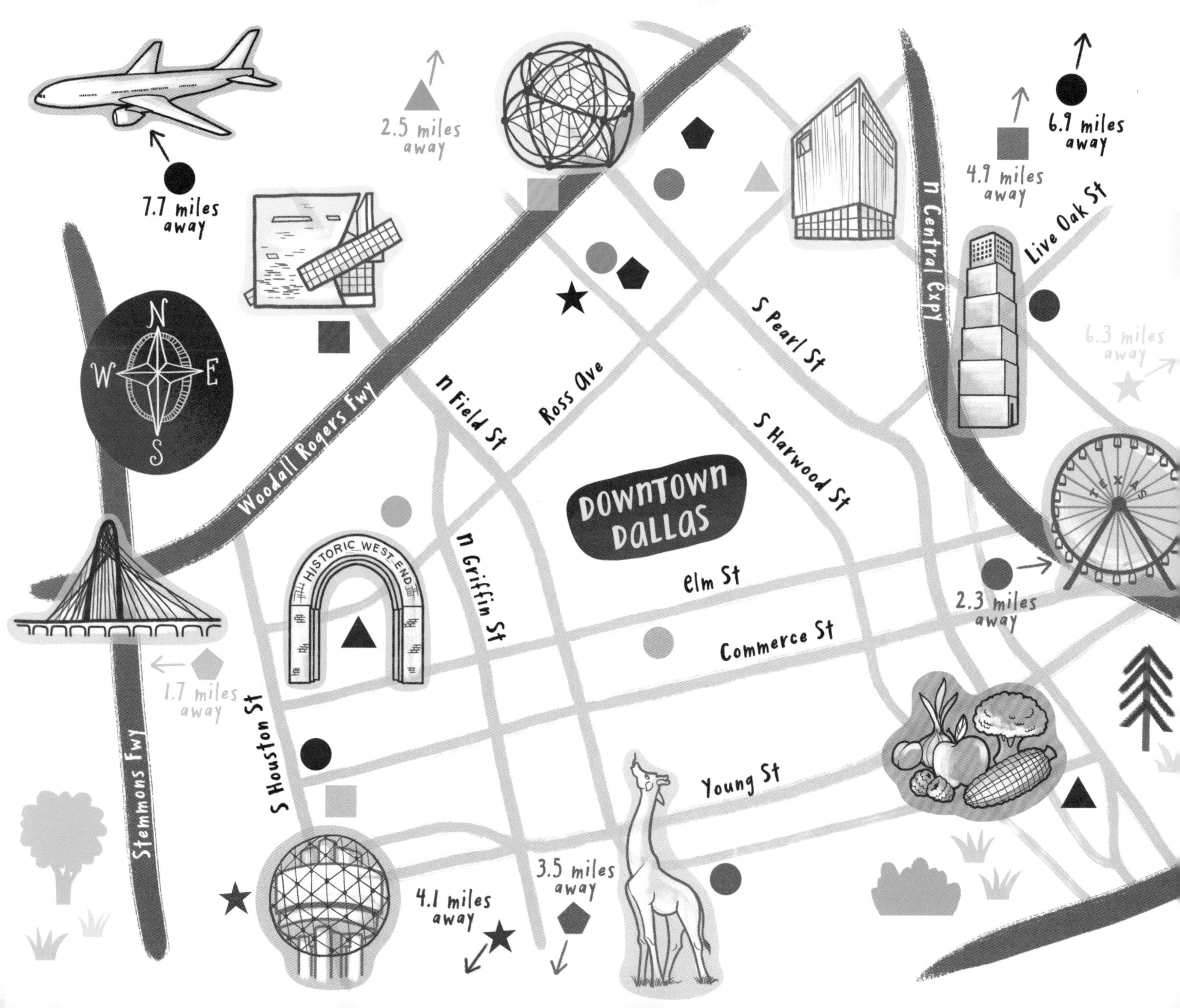

2.5 miles away
7.7 miles away
4.9 miles away
6.9 miles away
N
W
E
S
Woodall Rogers Fwy
N Field St
Ross Ave
S Pearl St
S Harwood St
N Central Expy
Live Oak St
6.3 miles away
DOWNTOWN DALLAS
HISTORIC WEST END
N Griffin St
Elm St
Commerce St
2.3 miles away
1.7 miles away
S Houston St
Stemmons Fwy
Young St
TEXAS
3.5 miles away
4.1 miles away

# LEGEND

- Perot Museum of Nature and Science
- Klyde Warren Park
- Dallas World Aquarium
- Nasher Sculpture Center
- Meyerson Symphony Center
- Winspear Opera House
- Wyly Theatre
- Crow Museum of Asian Art
- Dallas Museum of Art
- Margaret Hunt Hill Bridge
- Dallas City Hall
- Reunion Tower
- Magnolia Hotel and The Pegasus
- Old Red Museum
- Dallas County Courthouse
- Latino Cultural Center
- Dallas Farmer's Market
- Bishop Arts District
- Turtle Creek
- Southern Methodist University
- Dallas Zoo
- Fair Park
- Dallas Love Field Airport
- Dallas Arboretum and Botanical Garden
- NorthPark Center
- West End Historic District